Coastal Canada

Coastal Canada

Text by Kildare Dobbs

Discovery Books

(Pages 2-3) Campobello Island, N.B., once a summer retreat for Franklin D. Roosevelt.

(Page 4) The railroad to Squamish runs along Howe Sound.

Produced by Discovery Books for:
W. H. Smith,
Toronto, Canada

ISBN 0-919493-41-6

Photograph Credits

Paul von Baich pages 8-9, 106, 108, 132 (right).

Gera Dillon pages 19, 28-29, 90 (bottom).

Kildare Dobbs pages 24, 59.

Ken Elliott pages 36 (right), 55 (top), 92.

Menno Fieguth pages 37, 82, 98-99, 104, 105 (top), 107, 109 (right), 110, 117, 119, 122, 123, 124, 125, 126, 129, 131, 132 (left), 136, 139 (top), 141, 142, 143.

Richard Fyfe pages 68, 69, 83.

Tom Hall pages 134-135, 137, 144.

Lyn Hancock pages 4, 112, 113, 114, 118, 120, 121, 127, 133.

Bill Ivy pages 36 (left), 48 (bottom).

Thomas Kitchin pages 105 (bottom), 109 (left), 111, 115, 130.

John de Visser pages 12-13, 18, 22, 23, 25, 26, 30, 32, 34, 38-39, 40, 41, 42, 43, 44, 45, 46, 47, 49 (top), 51, 52-53, 54, 55 (bottom), 56-57, 60, 61, 62, 64, 65, 66-67, 70, 71, 72, 73, 74, 76-77, 78, 79, 80, 84, 85 (bottom), 89, 90 (top), 91, 93, 94, 96, 102, 116, 128, 138, 140.

Richard Vroom pages 2-3, 16, 20-21, 27, 31, 33, 48 (top), 49 (bottom), 50, 58, 63, 75, 81, 85 (top), 86-87, 88, 95, 97.

Dudley Witney pages 35, 139 (bottom).

Designed by Maher & Murtagh
Typesetting by Compeer Typographic Services Ltd.

Printed and bound in Italy by Sagdos S.p.A.

Contents

Introduction 8

Atlantic Canada 12

Pacific Canada 98

Introduction

The seacoast of Canada is unimaginably long: 243,798 kilometres (including island coastlines) from the border of Maine on the Atlantic, northward to the Arctic, and south again to the point where the border of Washington touches the Pacific Ocean.

Since the Arctic and sub-Arctic coasts are locked in perpetual ice, blurring the distinction between land and ocean in many places, we are concerned here only with the more accessible seacoasts of the Atlantic provinces and of British Columbia. In these coastal areas the frontiers of our northern kingdom have a geographical reality lacking in the straight line of the southern 49th parallel, originally drawn on a blank map by the arbitrary hands of negotiators schooled in Cartesian geometry. Along our coasts the limits of Canada have been carved for us by the actions of winds and tides, by convulsions of the earth's crust, and the advance and retreat of glaciers over eons of geological time.

The Fathers of our Canadian Confederation, together with their British Imperial godfathers in Westminster, conceived their as yet non-existent country on a scale of extraordinary, not to say immodest, grandeur. Since there was no word for a self-governing nation within an empire, they chose the word "dominion" from the prophetic sentence in one of the Psalms: "And he shall have dominion also from sea to sea."

In 1867 the Confederation began with only four provinces: Quebec, Ontario, Nova Scotia and New Brunswick. All were in the east, separated from the tiny Pacific settlements by a great void of prairies, a wall of immense mountains, and distances so great that the sun itself took four hours to traverse them. Yet the motto of Canada, veiled in Latin, was nevertheless a phrase from that same prophetic sentence: *A Mari usque ad Mare*. (From Sea even unto Sea.)

From the beginning, then, Canada was conceived as a nation with seacoasts on two oceans.

To many inland Canadians the sea is just the sea, one ocean like another, and sea-coasts in the same latitude much of a muchness. Not so. Canada's Atlantic shores are very different from those on the Pacific, especially the coasts sheltered by Vancouver Island. Atlantic winters bring heavy snow and harsh winds. Pacific winters are mild and rainy; snow is infrequent, except on the mountains; spring comes early. The forests of the eastern seaboard are unlike those of the west.

It is, however, in the perspectives of human culture and history that the regions most differ. European colonies began to take root on the Atlantic shores some three hundred years ago. In more than fifteen generations, Maritimers have evolved ways of living with each other and their environment, ways peculiar to themselves. They know their country and their coasts, the shoals and tidal rips, the changing seasons and weather.

(*Previous pages*) The port of Prince Rupert.

They have inherited certain habits and styles, not only in outlook and speech, but in the ways they build their houses and boats, cultivate their fields, and catch and cure their fish. Somewhat set in their ways, they cling to ethnic loyalties and hostilities, retaining ancestral languages, folkways, even feuds, while living side by side with others who do not share them.

In comparison with other Canadians, Maritimers are often poor; yet most are not disabled by material deprivation. Their self-respect, their sense of community and belonging are not shattered by hard times. On the contrary, hardship has brought them closer together, making them more conscious of their distinctness from other Canadians.

The Atlantic coasts seem part of an older, more disillusioned world than the rest of Canada. Although the region has resemblances to other Atlantic areas, to New England, on the American side, to Galicia, western Ireland and Scotland, on the European side, it remains a place apart. Western man has been on this coast long enough to feel he has always been here.

Long acquaintance with trade and seafaring has given Maritimers a sense of their place in the world. Europe, New England and the West Indies have been part of their experience as long as Quebec, and longer than anywhere west of that. The people of Boston must be ignorant, said the Nova Scotian bard James Gillis; though everyone in Baddeck knows where Boston is, no one in Boston knows where Baddeck is.

The historic perspective of Canadians living on the Pacific coast is very different. Europeans in significant numbers have been here perhaps six or seven generations at most. They can still marvel at their beautiful country as though scarcely used to it. Theirs is the excitement of pioneers learning to live in a new and virgin environment. A Pacific style in art and architecture is emerging, though still at the self-conscious stage, not yet a vernacular.

The Coast Mountains with their brooding forests are mysterious and a little menacing, part of a domain little known to townspeople and romantically called the Interior. There, as some devoutly believe, certain sylvan monsters have been glimpsed, specimens of the Sasquatch or Big Foot, cousin to the Abominable Snowman of the Himalayas.

Pacific people are at once more rational and more superstitious than Maritimers; or, to put it another way, more modern. The modern person, always in doubt about trivial matters, has no guide but reason. To settle these trivial questions by following tradition, as Maritimers tend to do, is more comfortable.

The Atlantic shore breeds ghosts; the Pacific, shamans and spirits. Maritimers have ancestors, the Pacific has old-timers. In the Maritime perspective, a century is not long; on the Pacific, it is halfway back to Adam and Eve.

Go to the Atlantic and you look back to Europe, the Old World, the rising sun. On the Pacific coast, the New World behind you now, you look out to gathering night and to limitless possibility, the end of a quest and the beginning of another.

Atlantic Canada

Coming to Canada by sea from the east, as the discoverers did, one is appalled by the dangers in the way. It is as though the elements did not want European man to arrive on these shores. The north Atlantic is a savage ocean, the grey widow-maker of sailors' nightmares. On a few clear days in summer the waves are still, the wind drops and the sea is a glassy lake. No one could imagine any harm in that tranquil expanse. Yet even on that kind of day, perhaps especially on that kind of day, the sailor is mistrustful, checking the barometer for signs of collapse, testing the wind in case it should be backing, always a bad omen.

More often the weather is boisterous, blowing half a gale (Force 7 on the Beaufort scale) as the light breaks through driving clouds, gusting on dancing water among the white-caps. Now the sailor moves with practiced caution, one hand for jack tar (himself) and the other for his employer, clutching a lifeline while he tends to his work.

And then, luckily not too often – though often enough to make the sailor wish he had chosen some other calling – there are hurricanes. A hurricane is hard to describe to land-lubbers or even to people who have been at sea in moderately heavy weather. There is nothing in ordinary experience that prepares one for it. The motion is violent beyond imagining, tons of water falling on the ship with a force that tears away steel upperworks, twists davits into fantastic shapes and smashes boats to shreds of matchwood. But the confusion is worse, of sky and sea, water and wind and light and dark: a vast, terrifying, impersonal savagery, a tumult of continuing crisis that goes on and goes on. Until at last the fragile lives are released miraculously with a sense that their survival is merely reprieve, a humorous whim of the elements.

Gales and hurricanes are only the Atlantic's first line of defence. The seas that coil around Canada's eastern approaches are often shrouded in fog. With radar the modern navigator can see through fog, but the blips are sometimes ambiguous and accidents still occur. In fog the sailor is content to make steerage-way, sounding a mournful horn at intervals, listening for the warning clang of a bell-buoy or the bleat of a groaner. Fog can be thin and deceptive, or so thick a man cannot see his hand in front of his face.

Then there is ice. The waters of the north Atlantic are invaded by a continual flow of icebergs and pack ice that drifts south on the Labrador current and eastward off the coast of Nova Scotia for hundreds of miles. The fate of the *Titanic* is warning enough of the dangers of ice.

And there are hazards like Sable Island, a long low sandspit lying some hundred miles off Nova Scotia, where in 1598 the French, incredibly, tried to plant a colony. Only eleven colonists survived. But, as though the wraiths of their dead comrades sought company,

(Pages 12-13) Shores carved by surf and wind, near Peggy's Cove, N.S.

ship after ship was wrecked in that unlucky place.

Finally, there are the rocky northeast coasts of Canada themselves, glowering ironbound outposts from the Avalon peninsula of Newfoundland to Labrador. Approaching St. John's in winter makes the heart sink. A wall of rugged cliffs is hung with stalactites of silver ice. One is close, too close as it seems, to the base of those walls, with ragged "sunkers" under water, and the waves raging and boiling around them, before the opening in the cliffs appears – the entrance to a completely sheltered harbor. How beautiful it is, this snow-bound seaport, dominated by the castle on top of Signal Hill, where Marconi received his first trans-Atlantic radio message! The wooden houses, painted and caulked and double-glazed against the weather, by night send their soft lamplight, echoed in the dark trembling water, to welcome the storm-beaten ships. In the grand cathedral, designed by George Gilbert Scott in Victorian times, in the clapboard churches and chapels, voices are raised in hymns of thanksgiving and supplication "for those in peril on the sea."

Jacques Cartier, who came to the shores of Labrador in 1534, called it "the land God gave to Cain," all "stones and horrible rugged rocks." Once safely through the fogs and storms off western Newfoundland, however, he found his way to the Gaspé peninsula in high summer. On the island of Anticosti he found strawberries, raspberries and gooseberry bushes. And wild dog-roses, the bonny briar rose that today brightens the roadside hedges of the region. He claimed the new country for France.

Newfoundland had been discovered, in a formal sense, by John Cabot in 1497. But the cod fisheries, based on the teeming abundance of the nearby Grand Banks, were already functioning. According to a letter written late in the same year by one Johan Day to a Spanish correspondent (in Spanish); Cabot's men "found many fish like those which in Iceland are dried in the open and sold in England and other countries, and those fish are called in England 'stockfish'." The earliest known reference to "stokfish" in English occurred in 1290; in 1436 there was a reference to "the comodius stockfysshe of Yselonde." If English fishermen were curing their fish in Newfoundland instead of Iceland, they did not admit it until after 1497. It was no different with the Bretons and Basques and Portuguese.

Europeans in any event had come to these coasts as early as 1000 A.D., when Leif Ericsson with a crew of thirty-five, as the Icelandic Sagas tell, explored the region. Landing in the place he called Helluland (Slabland), which seems to have been Baffin Island, he found it a worthless country. Markland (Forestland), which he came to next, was probably Labrador. Vinland (Wineland), where he established a short-lived colony, seems to have been Newfoundland. Archaeologists have discovered a site at L'Anse aux Meadows, Newfoundland, that answers to the description in the saga, with the remains of several houses, certain Viking artifacts, and a probable date of 1000 A.D. or so. The name L'Anse aux Meadows is a corruption of *L'anse aux méduses* (jellyfish cove) and the site is close to the Strait of Belle Isle. And yet the tribesmen of the area had no memory of those earlier migrants by the time the European fishermen began to arrive.

The French, who had access to plentiful and cheap supplies of sea-salt, practiced what became known as the green fishery. That is, they lavishly salted down their catches after cleaning them, and took them home in that form, a kind of pickled cod.

The English, following the Icelandic example, salted their catches only lightly. They then landed to split them and dry them on rocks, or on wooden racks called flakes. They used this method because salt was expensive in England. But eventually they found markets for their dry product in southern Europe which brought them such profit that the French began to practice the dry fishery too. Now that both English and French were landing on Newfoundland to dry their catches, colonization gradually followed.

The British, however, wanted Newfoundland to remain much as it was, to contribute to their growing sea power as a nursery of sailors – the best in the world. For long periods the only rule in Newfoundland was that of the Fishing Admirals, until the economic interests of French and English shifted from the Atlantic fisheries to the fur trade.

Saint John, New Brunswick, Canada's first incorporated city.

The first settlement in Canada was established by the French in the Bay of Fundy around a town they called Port Royal, now Annapolis Royal. The Acadian French are still there, after many cruel setbacks, including a period of expulsion in the 18th century.

The tidal pattern of the Bay of Fundy must be unique in the world. Here there is a prodigious rise and fall of tide, as the waters are constricted in the narrow bay. The difference between high and low water at spring tides is a good forty feet. When the tide flows, the sea rushes into the bay, covering the wide flats of shiny red mud, and gushing into the raw red beds of rivers that look, with their branching trunks and tributaries, like renderings of arteries in anatomical text-books. During the rum-running days of the 1920s boats laden with contraband would be run up these rivers and creeks at high water and hidden in the woods.

The Atlantic coast has always been haunted by pirates and smugglers. Some say the treasure of Captain Kidd is buried in one of the mysterious shafts that go down to tidal water on Oak Island. Despite many attempts no one has yet succeeded in finding the legendary booty.

But the real treasure of Atlantic Canada is the produce of the sea: cod, pollock, mackerel, herring, lobster, scallops, swordfish, shrimp, crab and mussels. Whatever plenty the Atlantic affords, it is found here. However, the men who go to sea in all weather do not earn the prices that fish bring in retail outlets far inland. During the hard times of the 1930s, the fishermen created cooperatives; as these succeeded, businessmen were attracted to the fish industry, killing the cooperatives with their competition. Now that times are hard again, the businessmen are failing, and this time there are no cooperatives to take up the tasks of processing and distribution. But fishing continues.

One of the loveliest things in these waters is the Cape Island fishing vessel, a flawless example of how function can perfect design. With its clean, curving lines from high bow to low stern, its roomy belly that defies the heavy seas, the craft has evolved over time under the hands of master-shipwrights. Along the seaward coast of Nova Scotia, New Brunswick and Gaspé, but especially at Lunenburg, N.S., shipwrights swing their adzes, squaring hardwood or softwood timbers cut in the nearby forests.

The same timber is used to build houses, ship-shape and Bristol fashion, painted in bright colors or a dazzle of black and white. Roads follow the coasts, bordered by pine and spruce; grassy fields run to the cliff's edge, where the white, clapboard lighthouse stands against blue sky. And from Gaspé to Fundy surf tumbles on beaches of white sand, here secreted in a cove, there – as at Dalvay Beach, Prince Edward Island – running for miles along a shore backed by grassy dunes.

Visitors come for these beaches and for the lobster. But the many historic sites of this down-home region of Canada are almost as strong an attraction, and some of them are in the cities: Saint John, New Brunswick; Halifax, Nova Scotia; and Charlottetown, Prince Edward Island.

Up for the winter, near Caraquet, N.B.

At Anse Beaufils, Gaspé, a fisherman un-
tangles his nets.

(*Overleaf*)
A golden hour on Cavendish
Beach, P.E.I.

Newfoundland gales are fierce. At Grand
Bruit even the church has to be tied down
with steel guys.

Winter seas spend their rage on the rocky
southwest coast of Newfoundland.

Ship-building on the Acadian shore.
Before steel hulls, Maritime yards helped
build British sea power.

The end of the voyage. Burgeo, Nfld.

Oyster digger's tools, Shediac, N.B.

Raking Irish moss, an edible seaweed
harvested at Tignish, P.E.I.

Friends and strangers at Cavendish Beach P.E.I.

On a shore near Cap Gaspé, Jacques Cartier planted the cross and *fleur-de-lys* of France in 1534.

This Canadian National coaster at
Makkovik, Labrador, is the sole link with
"outside."

Scallops raked from the sea-bed by P.E.I.
draggers.

Caribou moss and wintergreen on the
coast of Labrador.

Clams and more clams. Bideford, P.E.I.

(Right)
New London lighthouse, P.E.I.

In the hot summer of 1534, Cartier named
this *baie des Chaleurs.*

Pink Lady's Slipper or Moccasin Flower, floral emblem of Prince Edward Island.

Summer flowers in bloom beside a dory, on a Lunenburg beach in Nova Scotia.

A touch of autumn on Cape Breton
Island, N.S.

(*Overleaf*)
Boats are stowed above
tide-water for the severe Gaspé winter.

Newfoundland fishermen are the best
seamen in the world, handling a dory or a
whaler in any weather.

(Right)
Traditional lobster traps can be mended
without special tools. (N.B.)

Cape Breton, N.S. "Home is the sailor,
home from sea . . ."

Stowing a fine catch on the Grand Banks.

(*Left*) Nain, Labrador, in summer.

Inuit friends at Nain, Labrador.

Far out in the Gulf of
St. Lawrence, the Magdalens.

Labrador winter with huskies.

In Nova Scotia, man is not the only fisher.

Heavy weather off Cape Makkovik,
Labrador.

Smoked salmon fit for gourmets will result from this trip to a New Brunswick smokehouse.

The Pitcher Plant, Newfoundland's floral emblem.

Wild horses survive on Sable Island, where many a good ship foundered.

Loading the traps at Tignish,
Prince Edward Island.

Blue Rocks, Nova Scotia.

(*Right*)
Through most of its history the Gaspé was isolated from central Quebec and Canada. Near La Martre, Gaspé.

Cliffs of Cape St. Mary's, Nfld., are a sanctuary for nesting gannets.

Gaspé fishing vessel stranded at low tide.

No cod today. But how about a nice piece
of salmon? Sidewalk vendor in St. John's.

Growing up amphibious in Greenspond
Island, Newfoundland.

Old St. John's. Fishermen's houses at The Battery.

58

Loyalist refugees from the American colonies founded St. Andrews, New Brunswick.

Fish weir off Grand Manan Island, N.B.

One more river to cross. Upper
Pokemouche, New Brunswick.

Cows ruminate where 300 years ago men
built a settlement on the coast of
Newfoundland.

The rugged rocks of Tikkoatokak Bay,
Labrador.

(Right) Preparing bait at Blue Rocks, Nova Scotia.

In the delirium of spring the ocean
waits. . . . Humber Arm, Nfld.

Cold storage, old-style, at Wesleyville,
Newfoundland.

(*Overleaf*)
Dawn over Percé Rock, Gaspé.

A village in the lonely Magdalen Islands.

Idle hours in the Nova Scotia sun.

(Left)
In Peggy's Cove, N.S., fishermen net
more tourists than fish.

Drying fish in Newfoundland.
Flakes today are made of wire.

Fundy's forty-foot tides leave wide mud-flats.

(*Right*)
Codfish drying on wire flakes in the Gaspé will make stockfish.

Ice and iceberg in the Labrador Sea, with harp seals.

Blue Rocks, Nova Scotia.

(*Overleaf*)
Labrador Sea: Arctic ice moving south and east.

(*Top*) New Brunswick clam-diggers.

(*Bottom*) Colorful houses at
Cape St. Mary's, Nfld.

Rock forms at Digby Neck, N.S., resemble
the Giant's Causeway in Northern Ireland.

At work on a fish weir near Digby, N.S.

Just enough breeze to fill the sails in
Mahone Bay, Nova Scotia.

The Cabot Trail, Cape Breton Island.

A south coast outport. Newfoundlanders live almost in the sea.

Cape Spear, the easternmost point of
Newfoundland.

(*Top*) A quiet afternoon of fishing from a dock at Rustico, P.E.I.

(*Bottom*) Caribou on the southwest coast of Newfoundland.

(*Overleaf*)
P.E.I. lobster traps dry in the sun.

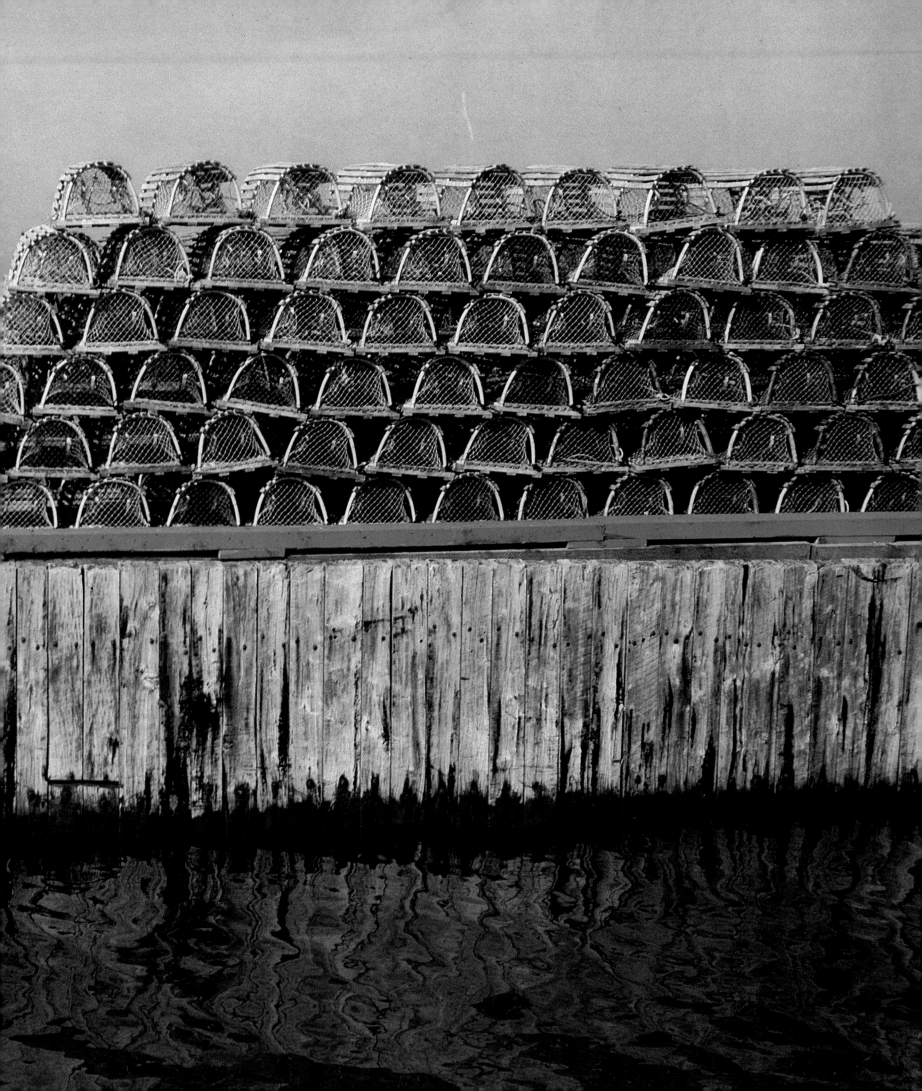

White sand, sun and sky at Brackley
Beach, P.E.I.

(Right)
Hopewell Rocks, sculpted by the
scouring tides of Fundy.

Lobster Point, P.E.I.

Cape Breton dawn.

Kaumajet Mountains, Labrador, "the land
God gave to Cain."

(*Left*)
Bluenose II, replica of Canada's pride of the
'20s and '30s.

François, Newfoundland, huddles at
the head of a mile-long fiord.

Hard, grey weather breeds hardy
seamen. Port aux Basques, Nfld.

(Right)
Winter grips Grand Manan Island
in the Bay of Fundy.

(Right)
Murray Harbour houses and boats are built with the same sure hands. (P.E.I.)

Access to North West River, Labrador, is by cable ferry.

Pacific Canada

The discoverers of Atlantic Canada were generally pleased with the land they found, reporting that it was beautiful, by which they meant suitable for cultivation. If they were wrong about the agricultural possibilities, which on the whole they were, despite the fine potato crops of Prince Edward Island, they are excused when one remembers that they were under an obligation to produce good news. Their expeditions had cost a lot of money. The investors deserved a rosy report or two.

It was different with the discoverers of Pacific Canada. They stressed the ardors and difficulties of their voyages and journeys. They were products of their age, an age of reason and classical regularity, and they did not find raw nature beautiful. In the 1790s Captain George Vancouver reported that "the shores put on a very dreary aspect, chiefly composed of rugged rocks, thinly wooded with small dwarf pine trees." North of the Gulf of Georgia he found "as gloomy and dismal an aspect as nature could well be supposed to exhibit." The trees, however, "screened from our sight the dreary rocks and precipices that compose these desolate shores."

To the 18th century eye, the very objects that excite the imagination of modern viewers – rocks, forests, mountains, cataracts, and landscapes from which humans are absent – were dismal and depressing. It was to take at least a century of romantic novels, poems and travel-writing to reverse this convention. Today one of the great attractions of Canada's Pacific coast is that it *is* wild and unspoiled; it has the qualities that travel advertisers call "scenic."

Most visitors land on this coast from the air at Vancouver. The city is blessed in its romantic site by the Pacific, sheltered from the turbulence of the open ocean by the barrier of Vancouver Island and the Gulf Islands scattered between. The bosky peninsula of Stanley Park juts into the sea; here are Douglas firs of immense size, as old as, or older than, any other living thing on earth. The gleaming modern city stands on the delta of the Fraser River in a valley dominated by the Coast Mountains. The air is mild and damp, warmed by the Japanese current that drifts this far on the surface of the Pacific. Vegetation is luxuriant and rank; the gardens are more than English with their trim, green lawns and herbaceous borders. A green, flowery place is Vancouver, with holly in the hedges and smooth-trunked arbutus by the gently lapping sea.

No place could be so green and fertile without rain. And there is plenty of rain, so that often the visitor is told, confronting an expanse of grey water, grey cloud and grey rain, that the view here is wonderful, of ships and mountains and yachts riding at moorings. None of this is evident, yet when the sun breaks through, a dazzle on the sea, light and color banish grey from the mind and imagination.

(*Pages 98-99*) Lions Gate Bridge, Vancouver, B.C.

Vancouver is a great seaport trafficking with the Orient and the whole world. Ocean freighters pass in and out under the great Lions Gate suspension bridge that spans Burrard Inlet. Their comings and goings do something to ease a certain sense of isolation induced by the wall of mountains on the north shore.

British Columbia lives largely by the export of resources: minerals, forest produce and fish. Herring are fished for conversion to fertilizer; shrimp, crab and other crustaceans and shellfish appear fresh on the tables of Vancouver and Victoria. Japanese oysters were introduced many years ago and are flourishing in coastal waters. But the most famous product of this coast is Pacific salmon. There are five species, all of them excellent for freezing or canning. They are spawned in the rivers, like Atlantic salmon, pass most of their lives in the ocean and return as adults to breed in the rivers in which they were spawned.

Europeans first came to the Canadian Pacific coast in the 18th century to trap sea otters and trade their pelts in the Orient. These beautiful animals were taken near to the point of extinction, though now they are protected and re-established in numbers large enough to ensure survival.

But Europeans were late-comers to this region. By the time they came, several native coastal tribes had developed a level of civilization that was impressive by any standard. Haida, Kwakiutl, Salish, Nootka and others built elaborately decorated dwellings from the splendid timber that grew around them, celebrating their lineage with lofty ancestral poles (totem poles) and their wealth in ceremonial entertainments called potlatches. They still practice their arts today. Antique pieces fetch astonishing prices in the auction rooms of New York, London and Paris.

The Strait of Georgia separates the mainland from Vancouver Island, site of the provincial capital, Victoria, which, with the naval base at Esquimalt, lies at the southern tip of the island. Beaches along both shores of the Strait of Georgia are littered with great logs that have escaped the rafts of various lumber companies. The Gulf Islands sometimes remind one of the Greek islands as they must have been in classic times when, it is said, pines from Pelion's crest swam through the clear waters of the Aegean:

Then, if ever with their own eyes mortals saw
Sea-nymphs start from the foam . . .

though in British Columbia no one but an imaginative beachcomber would make such a claim.

The neat, orderly world of Victoria, with its superlative gardens and conscious echoes of English suburbia, could blind one to the fact that Vancouver Island is a country in itself that has hardly been developed. A road runs along the eastern coast as far as Campbell River and beyond that to Kelsey Bay. But no one could get far by road along the west coast, where the great ground-swell of the Pacific Ocean, rolling all the way from China, breaks against the western limits of Canada.

Most of the island is covered in temperate rain forest, so thick

that no one could hope to cut his way through it without machinery.
Rainfall here is as much as three hundred inches a year. And that
means, as in western Scotland, that if you can see the mountains it is
going to rain; and if you cannot see them, it is raining already.

Between Tofino and Port Renfrew lies the Pacific Rim National
Park, a wilderness area of extraordinary fascination. Long Beach
stretches for miles. The white sandy beach is hard and densely packed
and at low tide is half a mile deep. The ocean here is rich in fish,
octopus and shellfish. Along this coast dolphins and sea lions abound,
killer whales are often seen, and all sorts of sea birds run along the
waterline or skim over the waves.

The Pacific, despite its name, can be as violent and destructive as
the Atlantic. The sky lowers and darkens, the entire horizon of ocean
seems to lift and fall as surf thunders on the shore with a sound like
heavy artillery firing a barrage. The wind tears and strains at the forest.
There are places along this coast where no roads run and no lifeboats
are stationed, where almost as many ships have foundered as have
broken their backs along the wreck-strewn passage of Magellan.
Most of the settlements along the Pacific coast are accessible only
by air or by sea. At Friendly Cove, a cairn commemorates the visit of

Cormorants hitch a ride off Queen Charlotte Islands.

Captain James Cook in 1778, on his last, fateful voyage. George Vancouver was with him, a midshipman at the time. He returned as a captain in 1791 to establish Britain's claim to the area over that of Spain.

After nearly 200 years the British and their Canadian successors have done surprisingly little to change the place. For the Pacific coast is still a Canadian wilderness. Settlers moved into the cosy valleys of the interior or the mild shores of the Straits of Georgia. Miners and loggers did venture into the wild country, but only to plunder and take away its resources. Notions of conservation and husbandry were slow to develop.

It was not until the 1950s that Canadian aluminum smelting installations were erected at Kitimat at the head of Douglas Channel, the beginning of a small community that also worked at logging. This settlement and the grain harbor and fishing center at Prince Rupert, some thirty miles south of the Alaska panhandle, are still about the only signs of effective occupation to be found on the coast of northern British Columbia.

There is a Russian story of a man who is offered all the land he can run around in a single day. He runs so far, encompassing so much land that the effort kills him. The story is called "How Much Land Does A Man Need?" Maybe something like that happened with Canadians; they put forth such a mighty effort in staking their claim *A Mari usque ad Mare* that there was little energy left for nation-building. Today some 26 million people inhabit this great empty land, most of them unwilling to stray more than a hundred miles north of the U.S. border. The excuse is that much of the land is useless. The strange thing is that this is happening in a time when technology-happy experts predict the founding of human colonies in space.

One benign result of this sovereign neglect is that in the rock pools along the Pacific coast, tiny Edens may still be found, minute ecologies in which snail, seaweed, crab, anemone, mussel, minnow, and tiny starfish survive, with mutual benefit, from tide to tide. In a world that has lost its innocence, those crystal-clear gardens of marine life may be the only Edens left.

The mysterious past: petroglyph at Grove
Island.

Flowers bloom in Beacon Hill Park,
Victoria, B.C.

Abandoned fishing-boat at Southland.

Coasts from which man is absent, near
Stewart, B.C.

Industrial installations at Indian Arm.

(*Left*)
Shore of Stanley Park, Vancouver.

Shangri-la on the Pacific: West Vancouver,
British Columbia.

Dome of the legislature in spring at
Victoria, B.C.

Low tide at South Pender: a heron dries his
wings.

Snow geese in the Fraser estuary.

In between rain storms at Princess Louisa Inlet.

A Gulf Islands cougar keeps a dry tail.

Leather starfish and sun starfish.

(*Right*)
Salmon fishing is a vital industry of British Columbia.

Smoke rises above a Kwakiutl settlement at
Alert Bay, B.C.

A tall totem returns to earth in the coastal forest.

A pristine ecology, with sea-urchins and starfish.

Working logs at Beaver Cove, B.C.

(*Left*)
West coast of Vancouver Island at Barkley
Sound: a little-known Canada.

Abandoned riches. Driftwood at Nelson
Island.

Life is good for lotus-eaters with cedar, sun
and hot-tubs on Berry Island, near Port
Hardy, B.C.

Squamish is at the head of Howe Sound.

(Right) Vancouver from Queen Elizabeth Park.

Marina at Nanaimo on Vancouver Island.

Fresh fillets at Nanaimo.

(*Overleaf*)
An island lake to dream of. Buttle Lake,
Vancouver Island.

128

(*Previous page*)
A bald eagle fishes for spawning salmon,
Vancouver Island.

(*Left*)
The female deity, Tsonoqua, at Alert Bay.   Blessed sun at Courtenay, B.C.

(Left)
Beauty with a humble name – skunk
cabbage.

Temperate rain forest in the Pacific Rim
National Park.

The ferry at Horseshoe Bay, Howe Sound.

(*Left*)
The end of the road at Kelsey Bay,
Vancouver Island.

A female sea otter. In the late 1700s
fur-traders hunted this beautiful animal
almost to extinction.

(*Overleaf*) Dunes inshore from Long
Beach, Vancouver Island.

(*Left*)
The sands of Long Beach, Vancouver Island.

A northern bull sea lion on the Pacific coast with part of his harem.

(*Left*)
Taking it easy in Victoria Harbour.

Heavy nets, scant population at Prince Rupert's Port Edmond.

Vancouver boat-houses.

A catch of prime halibut.

Intimations of sausages at Coal Harbour,
British Columbia.

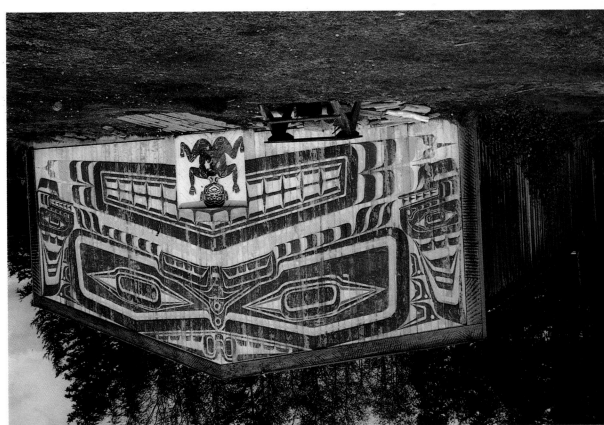

A Kwakiutl longhouse near Alert Bay.

Coming home to Gold River on
Vancouver Island.

(*Overleaf*)
Rain forest north of Victoria.